I0016409

100+ Frequently Asked Interview Question and Answers in Robotic Process Automation (RPA)

99% Frequently Asked Interview Q & A

By Bandana Ojha

Introduction

This book contains 100+ frequently asked interview questions in Robotic Process Automation (RPA) with short and straight forward answers.

Rather than going through comprehensive, textbook-sized reference guides, this book includes only the information required to start his/her career as a robotic process automation developer or tester. Answers of all the questions are short and to the point.

We assure that you will get here the 90% frequently asked interview questions and answers. It will help both freshers as well as experienced web developers.

1.What is Robotic Automation Process?

Robotic process automation (RPA) is a business process automation technology in which the robots simulate and mimic human actions for executing tasks without any human intervention in a business process.

2. What are the popular RPA tools?

The most popular RPA tools are:

Blue Prism: It is a trading name of the Blue Prism Group, a UK multinational software corporation, the term Robotic Process Automation was invented by Blue Prism, that it turns out they are the innovators in RPA Software development.

Automation Anywhere: Automation anywhere is another top RPA seller providing strong and User-friendly RPA tools to automate any complex tasks.

UiPath: UiPath is a Windows desktop Robotic Process Automation (RPA) Software, which is used for automation for various web, desktop and Citrix applications.

Other Popular tools are Pega, Nice and Workfusion.

3. What are the characteristics of RPA?

Code Free: RPA doesn't require programming skills. Employees with any subject expertise can be trained to automate RPA tools instantly. The whole work revolves around RPA chart which provides a flowchart designer to graphically link, drag and drop icons to represent steps in a process.

User-Friendly: RPA adoption originates within business operations rather inside IT departments. RPA projects require less IT skills and less investment. Eventually, the automation is lowered at a substantial rate.

Non- Disruptive: RPA avoids complexity and risk.

4. What is RPA life cycle?

RPA life cycle is defined in 4 phases:

Analysis: This is the beginning phase of the RPA lifecycle which analyzes the business processes for RPA development.

Bot Development: Development team works on fulfilling the requirements for the automation tasks.

Testing Phase: Development team performs quality checks for bots.

Deployment and Maintenance: Bot is deployed and maintained by the team.

5. List the Advantages of Robotic Process Automation.

Faster: The robots are responsible to carry out the execution here, thus a great measure of work can be performed quickly within a relatively short period and with accuracy.

Cost Effective: Robots can operate 24/7 and take no leave, when compared to humans. Thus, it is a cost-effective technique.

Consistency: It is a safe, non-invasive technology that doesn't obstruct with the inherent systems and provides flawless consistency of work to perform the activities.

Accuracy & Quality: RPA offers more dependable services to processes that possess a high probability of human error and so the accuracy is increased. Robots are more reliable, consistent and do not complain when expected to work tirelessly.

Increased Customer Satisfaction: The customer satisfaction can be gained by providing better quality of work with finest accuracy, and thus enhanced customer/client interaction leads to increased customer and client satisfaction.

6. What are the limitations of Robotic Process Automation?

Limitations of RPA:

-RPA cannot read any data that is non-electronic with unstructured inputs.

-RPA is not a cognitive computing solution. It cannot learn from experience and therefore has a 'shelf life'.

-Applying RPA to a broken and inefficient process will not fix it. RPA is not a Business Process Management solution and does not bring an end-to-end process view from approaches.

7. What is the primary goal of the RPA process?

The main object behind the development of the RPA process helps you to replace the repetitive and tedious tasks performed by humans, with the help of a virtual workforce.

8. What is RPA Designation?

The RPA designation signifies a great credential to that work with fixed present also defined compensation plans or signifies associated including the administration of plan assets.

9. What is BOT?

A software bot is a program designed to automate tasks. Typically, these tasks are simple, repetitive and routine. So, a software bot can perform them quicker and more efficiently than a human could. A bot is a software helper that supports, simulates and sometimes replaces human work.

10. What are the different types of bots?

Below are the different types of bots

-Task Bot(.atmx)

-META BOT(.mbot)

-IQ BOT

-Chat Bots

11. What is an Unattended bot?

An unattended bot is a bot that runs on a dedicated workstation (virtual machine) or (Virtualized Desktop)

12. How to create RPA Bot?

To create RPA bot, you need to follow these steps:

Record a task

Completed the bot implementation

Test the bot

Upload the bot the perform the automation.

13. How is a chatbot different from robotic process automation?

Chatbot – A computer program designed to simulate conversation with human users, especially over the Internet.

RPA (Robotic Process Automation) – A bot programmed to automate a manual business process of executing a task or an activity within a business function. A business function can be like HR/Finance/Procurement etc.

14. What is the difference between Thin Client & Thick Client?

Thin Client	Thick Client
Easy to deploy as they require no extra or specialized software installation	More expensive and more work to be done to deploy
Needs to validate with the server after data capture	Data verified by client not server
If the server goes down, data collection is halted as the client needs constant communication with the server	Only needs intermittent communication with server
Reduced security threat	Increased security issues

15. What is the difference between traditional automation and RPA?

Traditional Automation is long drawn and requires considerable manpower, time, effort and substantial cost.

RPA is a quick fix to instantly generate improvements.

Both traditional automation and RPA need solid strategy and planning but the implementation of RPA is a bit quicker.

While both are aimed towards the common goal of Automation, RPA is faster, better and cheaper than traditional automation.

16. What are the things to be taken care in the process of RPA Implementation?

-Define and focus on the desired ROI

-You should target to automate important and highly impactful processes

-Combine attended and unattended RPA

17. What are the steps you should follow to implement Robotic Process Automation?

Six steps to be followed for a successful RPA implementation are:

-Identify the Automation Opportunities

-Optimize the Identified Processes

-Build a Business Case

-Select the RPA Vendor of your choice

-Model RPA Development

-Start Continue Building Expertise RPA bots

18. What is screen scraping in RPA?

Screen scraping involves capturing bitmap data from the screen and cross-checking it against stored information to interpret it.

19. What are the benefits of screen scraping?

Here, are some major benefits of screen scraping:

-Works on the application which are not accessible even using UI frameworks

-Offers test digitization through Optical character

-Easy to implement & mostly accurate

20. How does screen scraping work?

The Screen Scraping Tool can handle both individual text elements, groups of text and blocks of text. One good example is when you are trying to scrape text in table format in an application. The Screen Scraping Tool automatically detects regions on the screen.

21. How is RPA different from other enterprise automation tools?

RPA allows organizations to automate at a fraction of the cost and time previously encountered. RPA is also non-intrusive in nature and leverages the existing infrastructure without causing disruption to underlying systems, which would be difficult and costly to replace. With RPA, cost efficiency and compliance are no longer an operating cost but a byproduct of the automation.

22. How does Robotic Process Automation work?

RPA robots are capable of mimicking many–if not most–human user actions. They log into applications, move files and folders, copy and paste data, fill in forms, extract structured and semi-structured data from documents, scrape browsers, and more.

23. What is Information Collection in RPA?

Information collection in RPA is collecting and measuring information from different resources and possibly providing them to robots to execute their operations easily and reliably.

24. What is Citrix automation process?

Citrix automation process is used to automate tasks such as filling fields and submitting the forms in the virtual desktop applications. Moreover, we can process the data entry form filling using Citrix automation.

25. What type of processes are suitable for Robotic Automation?

Best projects for robot automation are bulk repetitive rules-based procedures. The flexibility of the robotic automation platform is such that it does not matter if this involves interaction with multiple systems. You can see example processes that have built by our customers with our support in the Industries section of the website.

26. How long does a robot automation project take?

Typical projects are measured in weeks. One heuristic is that it takes as long to train a robot as it does a human. Complex new task will take longer depending of the level of object re-use available.

27. How easy is it to train and manage the robot's activity?

-A robot is trained through a flow chart of the procedure. This flow-chart is managed and audited to document the procedure.

-Management information is gathered automatically as the robot operates. All processes generate statistical profiles as a by-product of doing the action. This allows tuning and development of a process considering real data.

-Modern robots systems come with failover and recovery inbuilt as core capabilities. It means that if changes take place, or downstream failures occur a "smart" response can be trained into the overall system.

-Modern robots systems have full audit and security authorization meaning that all changes and all access is recorded and regulated. Back-up process steps are managed, roll-back and recovery, as well process change-highlighting, are all automatically captured by the robot platform.

28. How do robots deal with human judgment?

Robots for now only follow rules. Where a procedure requires interpretation and skill in judging an outcome then a robot may not be suitable. One technique that is common is to re-organize task-steps so that any judgment is dealt with up front – the work is prepared for robotic automation. In this way robots can handle bulk rules and hand off to humans once judgment is needed.

29. What is Automation Anywhere?

Automation Anywhere offers powerful and User-friendly Robotic Process Automation tools to automate tasks of any complexity.

30. How many types of variables are there in AA?

There are two types of applications in Automation Anywhere:

1.   System Variable

2.   Local Variable

31. What are the primary components of AA architecture?

Automation Anywhere Architecture has 3 primary components

-Control Room

-Bot Creator

-Bot Runner

32.What are the main features of AA?

Features of Automation Anywhere

-Intelligent automation for business and IT tasks

-Uses SMART Automation Technology

-Rapidly Automates complex and complicated tasks

-Create automation tasks like recording keyboard strokes and mouse clicks

-Distribute tasks to multiple computers

-Automation Anywhere offers script less automation

-Auto-login runs scheduled tasks on anytime, even when the computer is locked.

33. Why Automation Anywhere is popular?

Automation anywhere tool is popular because of the following reasons:

-No programming knowledge is required. You can record your actions or point and click the action wizards.

-Eliminates the element of the human error

-Increases transaction speed and allows to save time and costs

-Quick Time to Value, Non-intrusive

-Helps you to automate data transfers and import or export data between files or applications.

-Scale from Desktop to Data Center

34. What is Control room?

Control room is a web-based platform that controls the Automation Anywhere. In other words, it's the Server that controls Automation Anywhere bots.

35.What are Control room functions?

These are the control room functions

   -Operation manager

   -User Management

   -Audit trail

   -Bot scheduling

   -Bot versioning

   -License management

36. What is bot creator in Automation Anywhere?

Bot Creators are simply used to create bots. These are desktop-based applications whose sole role is to upload or download bots and connect them to the control room.

37. What is bot runner?

Bot Runners are responsible to run or execute the scheduled bots. Multiple bots can be executed in parallel, but the Bot Runners cannot update or create automation. This component of the Automation Anywhere is also connected to the Control Room and can report back the execution log status to the control room.

38. What is bot insights?

It is a tool that shows statistic and display graphs to analyze the performance of every bot in the system.

39. What is Bot Farm?

Bot Farm is integrated with Automation Anywhere Enterprise. It allows you to create multiple bots. Moreover, you can also give these boats on the rental basis.

40. What are Task Bots?

Task bots are bots which automate rule-based, repetitive task, in areas like document administration, HR, claims management, IT services and more. This leads to immediate improvement in productivity, error reduction, and cost saving.

41. What are Meta Bots?

Meta bots are the automation building blocks. It is designed in such a way that with application updates or changes you need to make minimal edits to the bot. Changes automatically apply to any process utilizing that bot.

42. What is IQBOT?

It is an advanced tool. It can learn on its own and perform a task according to it. IQ Bot offers automation using the highly advanced cognitive technology. It works on the concept to organize an unstructured data while improving its skills and performance.

43. What is RPA Blue Prism?

Blue Prism is an RPA Tool which holds the capability of virtual workforce powered by software robots. This helps the enterprises to automate the business operations in an agile and cost-effective manner. The tool is based on Java Programming Language and offers a visual designer with drag and drop functionalities.

44. What are Blue Prism Components?

The four main components of Blue Prism are:

Process Diagram

Process Studio

Object Studio

Application Modeler

45. What are the advantages of Blue Prism?

Blue Prism offers the following benefits:

Better Service Quality: As end-to-end auditing is performed by the Digital workforce; this tool offers a better service quality.

High Accuracy: This tool performs tasks in such a way that outcomes are produced with high accuracy and low errors.

Scalable: Provides a scalable approach, as this tool is not based on scripts or recorders but is based on intelligent Digital Workforce performing tasks.

Quick Deployment of Services: The services can be easily deployed as it can automate the application's controls, irrespective of their onscreen position.

Flexible Workforce: The Digital Workforce is designed in such a way that it doesn't need rest. It can work 24*7 without taking a break and give the same results with high accuracy.

Statistics: This tool offers dashboards so that you can analyze the data, the process's session and much more.

46. Is Blue Prism's Robotic Automation Platform secure and auditable?

Security and auditability are built into the Blue Prism robotic automation platform at several levels. The runtime environment is separate to the process editing environment. Permissions to design, create, edit and run processes and business objects are specific to each authorized user.

A full audit trail of changes to any process is kept, and comparisons of the before and after effect of changes are provided. The log created at run-time for each process provides a detailed, time-stamped history of every action and decision taken within an automated process.

47. What hardware infrastructure is needed to run Blue Prism's Robotic Automation Platform?

Blue Prism has been designed for flexibility and to meet the most robust IT standards for IT operational integrity, security, and supportability. The software can be deployed either as a front office or back office process, running quite happily on a standard desktop in the front office or on any scale of systems for back-office processing.

48. What Is Process Studio?

A Blue Prism Process is created as a diagram that looks much like a common business flow diagram.

Processes are created in an area of Blue Prism named Process Studio which, as we will see, looks like other process modeling applications (such MS Visio) and uses standard flow diagram symbols and notation.

49. What is UiPath?

UiPath is a Robotic Process Automation tool which is used for Windows desktop automation. It is used to automate repetitive/redundant tasks and eliminates the human intervention. The tool is simple to use and has a drag and drop functionality of activities.

50.How do you publish a code in UiPath?

The following are the steps to be followed to publish a workflow in UiPath: First, open UiPath Studio, create a new project, and give it an appropriate name. Go to the SETUP Ribbon and click on the Publish button.

51. What is state machine in UiPath?

A State Machine is a type of automation that uses a finite number of states in its execution. It can go into a state when it is triggered by an activity, and it exits that state when another activity is triggered. They also enable us to add conditions based on which to jump from one state to another. These are represented by arrows or branches between states.

52.What is a single block activity in UiPath?

Single Block Activity is the smallest type of project which is mainly called as Sequence. They are suitable for linear processes as they enable you to go from one activity to another seamlessly, and act as a single block activity. They can be reused time and again, as a standalone automation or as part of a state machine or flowchart.

53. What is the Assign activity in UiPath?

The Assign activity is an important activity that is going to be used quite often, as it enables you to assign a value to a variable. You can use an Assign activity to increment the value of a variable in a loop, sum up the value of two or more variables and assign the result to another variable, assign values to an array and so on. By default, this activity is also included in the Favorites group. To remove it, right-click it and select Remove.

54. What is the difference between UiPath and Selenium?

Selenium is specifically designed to test web applications and websites; it is impossible in selenium to interact with multiple applications and taking the output of one application as an input for other application. It cannot work with Virtual environments like Citrix at all.

UiPath is an RPA tool which is designed to automate any type of existing software process to replace any type of activities that can be performed by a human. So we can say that RPA is the next level of existing automation tools. It allows people to build a very complex rules-based process with very little software development skills. You can do all things using UliPath which can be done by Selenium but vice-versa is not possible.

55. What is Project Debugging in UiPath?

Debugging is the process of identifying and removing errors from a given project. Coupled with logging, it becomes a powerful functionality that offers you information about your project and step-by-step highlighting, so that you can be sure that it is error-free. Logging enables you to display details about what is happening in your project in the Output panel. This, in turn, makes it easier for you to debug an automation. Breakpoints enable you to pause the execution of a project so that you can check its state at a given point.

56. In UiPath studio, how elements are recognized on screen?

They can be recognized through the attributes of UI elements.

57. What are Arguments in UiPath?

Arguments are used to pass data from a project to another. In a global sense, they resemble variables, as they store data dynamically and pass it on. Variables pass data between activities, while arguments pass data between automation. As a result, they enable you to reuse automation time and again. UiPath Studio supports many argument types, which coincide with the types of variables. Therefore, you can create Generic Value, String, Boolean, Object, Array, or DataTable arguments and you can also browse for .NET types, just as you do in the case of variables. Additionally, arguments have specific directions (In, Out, In/Out, Property) that tell the application where the information stored in them is supposed to go.

58. What are the different types of recordings available in UiPath?

UiPath provides five different types of recordings according to requirement of the tasks:

1. Basic Recording
2. Desktop Recording
3. Web Recording
4. Image Recording
5. Native Citrix

59. When to use Basic recording in UiPath?

It is best suitable for recording single activities like opening or closing an application, selecting a checkbox etc. Basic recorder generates a full selector for each activity and no container. So, the resulted automation gets slower.

60. When to use Desktop Recording in UiPath?

It is suitable for every type of desktop apps and multiple actions or activities. Desktop Recorder generates a container, which encloses activities, and partial selectors for each activity. Thus, the resulted automation is faster than basic recording.

61. When to use web Recording in UiPath?

As the name suggests, web recording is used to record web apps and browsers. It generates containers and uses Simulate Type or Click input method.

62. When to use Image Recording in UiPath?

It allows only image, text and keyboard automation and requires explicit positioning. Image recording tool supports only Manual recording i.e. single actions. It is mainly used to record virtual environments like Virtual machines, Citrix etc.

63. When to use Citrix Recording in UiPath?

Native Citrix is used only in native Citrix environments and enables you to automatically record multiple actions performed on screen. It is equivalent of the Desktop recorder, but for Citrix environments. You can also manually record single actions.

64. Explain Append Range in UiPath?

Append range are used to Edit or Insert data into an existing workbook, with using of append range we can insert the data after the last written data from the workbook. Whenever we do append the data it will not overwrite the existing data.

65. What is the use of Element Exists?

It's used to identify the UI Element is present or not during the execution.

The output of the active support only Boolean.

66. What are Selectors and Wildcards in UiPath?

Wildcrafts helps in supplanting the strings. It is useful when you will manage the characteristics which are changing progressively in the selector.

What's more, the selector helps in naturally creating the determination by utilizing the wildcraft.

67. What is the Switch Activity in UiPath?

The Switch activity enables you to select one choice out of multiple, based on the value of a specified expression.

By default, the Switch activity uses the integer argument, but you can change it from the Properties panel, from the TypeArgument list.

The Switch activity can be useful to categorize data according to a custom number of cases.

68. What are contentions in UiPath?

Contention encourages the program to makes a few contentions where you can likewise roll out a few improvements. In contentions, you need to specify the name which is required. Expound on the course and select the contention-type whether they are a string, protest, Int 32 or cluster.

69. What is state machine in UiPath?

At the point when a machine is utilizing a specific number of states for computerization amid the execution, it is known as the state machine. It will just change starting with one state then onto the next if any action is activated.

70. What is venture investigating in UiPath?

Investigating is utilized for recognizing and demonstrating the mistake for a specific undertaking. It has breakpoints and logging and it is a sort of amazing usefulness which will assist you with gathering data about the task and will feature the blunders well ordered. Logging encourages you to realize what your activities are experiencing when the writing computer programs is done and is appeared in the yield board. Which helps in making the way toward investigating less demanding. While breakpoints help in stopping the execution of your undertaking to causes you to check the condition of the program at a specific point.

71. What is distributing a computerization venture implies in UiPath?

Distributing of the mechanization bundle shows filing it and the related documents present specifically organizer for sending it to robots and after that executing it. When you will be associated with the orchestrator then the venture will go to the orchestrator field and afterward it will be shown on bundles page. Furthermore, from this place, you can without much of a stretch disperse them to alternate robots after you relegate a few bundles to the earth. Else, it will get put away locally in the studio feed.

72. What is Do While Activity in UiPath?

The Do While activity enables you to execute a specified part of your automation while a condition is met. When the specified condition is no longer met, the project exits the loop.

This type of activity can be useful to step through all the elements of an array or execute a activity multiple time. You can increment counters to browse through array indices or step through a list of items.

73. What is the Delay Activity in UiPath?

Uipath utilizes the defer movement for making you delay or stop the computerization for some period. This is primarily utilized in ventures where you require great planning like pausing and afterward beginning of some specific applications or sitting tight for data preparing which you can use in the diverse action.

74. What is the If Activity in UiPath?

If movement is utilized when you will manage two conditions where the primary proclamation will get executed if the condition is valid while the second one will get executed when the announcement will be false. At the point when the variable will have values then the if proclamation is fundamentally utilized.

75. What is the break activity in UiPath?

The Break activity enables you to stop the loop at a chosen point, and then continues with the next activity.

76. Difference Between screen scraping and data scraping?

Screen scraping	Data scraping
Used to extract non-Structure data	Used to extract the structured data
Scraped information stored in String	Scraped information stored in Data table
Cannot easily extract the data into excel or DB	Can extract the data to excel or DB easily
Can extract image and pdf	Cannot extract from image and PDF

77. What is application navigator?

Application Modeler contains a feature called application navigator which provides a tree view of all the accessibility elements available within the application so that they can be easily found and selected.

78. What are selectors in Uipath?

The selector is a string of characters (VB expression) used to identify objects on the screen. The selector is one of the properties of UI activities and has an XML format. All the activities in UiPath Studio related to graphical elements have the selector property.

79. Can you store a selector in a variable?

Selectors are stored in the Properties panel of activities, under Input > Target > Selector. All activities related to graphical elements have this property. The Selector Editor window enables you to see the automatically generated selector and edit it and its attributes.

80.What is a wildcard selector?

Wildcard selector is used to select multiple elements simultaneously. It selects similar type of class name or attribute and use CSS property. * wildcard also known as containing wildcard.

81. What is the difference between RDA and RPA?

RDA is an automation solution that assists the agent in handling simple repetitive tasks. The agent plays a role in facilitating when the automation is triggered and stopped depending on their workflow.

The RPA is a headless operation in comparison. There are no agents to instruct the robot when to collect the information. There are no users interacting with the robot. The design of the automation is totally self-sustaining.

82. How is Chabot different from RPA?

A chatbot is a bot programmed to chat with a user like a human being while RPA is a bot programmed to automate a manual business process of executing a task or an activity within a business function.

83. What is PEGA automation?

Pega robotics adds the ability to automate tasks using the user interface of existing applications. It can help speed up manual tasks by automating user actions. Automations are created in Pega Robotic Studio. The latest version available is 8.0 and can be downloaded from PDN.

84. What is PGP?

Pretty Good Privacy (PGP) is an encryption program that provides cryptographic privacy and authentication for data communication. PGP is used for signing, encrypting, and decrypting texts, e-mails, files, directories, and whole disk partitions and to increase the security of e-mail communications.

85. For an Agile method, when you will not use automation testing?

If your requirements are frequently changing or your documentation becomes massive, then it is better to avoid automation testing method.

86. What is Attended Automation?

An attended automation bot is a bot that executes its automation on the user's local workstation

Attended bots can be invoked in

RPA products client tool

Embedded screen button

Existing screen UI element

87. What is the difference between Attended Automation vs Unattended Automation?

Attended Automation – BOTS will execute the task before the user/developer and manual intervention / input might be required from user.

Unattended Automation – BOTS will execute the tasks in background and its designed to work without users help

88. What are the various options available for error handling when an error occurs?

Err Number – to give error number which is uniquely tell the error type

Err Description – gives the description of the error

Continue/exit task

Take snapshot

Log

Send email

Variable assignment

Run another task

89. What is PGP?

Pretty Good Privacy or PGP is a popular program used to encrypt and decrypt email over the Internet, as well as authenticate messages with digital signatures and encrypted stored files.

90.What are uses of PGP encryption?

PGP encryption is to confidentially send messages. To do this, PGP combines private-key and public-key encryption. The sender encrypts the message using a public encryption algorithm provided by the receiver. The receiver provides their personal public-key to whomever they would like to receive messages from. This is done to protect the message during transmission. Once the recipient receives the message, they use their own private-key to decode the message, while keeping their personal private-key a secret from outsiders.

91. What is element mask?

Element mask is future in application modeler that enable you to copy the attribute selection of one element and apply it to another.

92. What are the Difference between Manage Windows/Web controls and Object Cloning?

Manage windows – lets you minimize / maximize /activate/close desktop-based application windows

Web Controls – lets you to perform operations like click some elements/set some values in text boxes/extract values from web elements and to open close browsers/navigate to URL. Basically, it's completely interacts only with web applications

Object cloning – lets you to perform operations like click some elements/set some values in text boxes/extract values from elements of both web and desktop applications

93. What is meant by Email automation?

Email automation there is no options to send email through email automation.

It only receives the messages.

There are two server types in email automation

IMAP

POP3

Three options will be there

All

Read

Unread

94. Name different types of Default Logs

Six types of Default logs are:

    -Execution start

    -Execution end

    -Transaction start

    -Transaction end

    -Error log

-Debugging log

95. What is Surface Automation?

Surface automation typically means virtual automation using screenshots, image recognition, and OCR.

96. What are the main components of RPA Solution Architecture?

Below are the components of RPA solution architecture

-Enterprise applications such as ERP Solutions (SAP)

-RPA tools – In any environment such as Citrix, web or desktop

-RPA Platform – Scheduling, distributing & monitoring the execution of software bots.

-RPA Execution Infrastructure

-Configuration management

97. Does a robot automation project require a specialist development environment?

No, as robots are trained in the live environment the traditional enterprise IT development environment is not required. Instead a robot is trained in the live environment just as user would be. Before active commit the robot is monitored through all its procedural steps with MI and monitoring tools to validate the procedure. The first stage of go-live can be set on "trickle" speed to ensure that procedures are acting according to requirements. Once output is cleared the process can be "accelerated" to mass automation speed.

98. What are the differences between Blue Prism and UiPath?

UiPath and Blue Prism both the tools have their respective software/Studio and they are very good. UI and BP both have visual process designers for developing the solutions.

Differences:

In terms of programming languages:

Blue Prism Uses C# for coding

UiPath uses VB for coding

In terms of Control Room/Dashboard

UiPath control room - The Orchestrator - is web based, you can access it from the browser or mobile.

BP have client-based servers, accessible only through their apps.

In terms of cost and uses:

UiPath:

Lower cost of development

Easier to learn and operate

You can learn by your self

Study materials are easily available on internet

Blue Prism:

Good for mass scale deployment of large number of robots

Higher cost of acquiring and using BP

Limited training available as the only source of training is BP

Training cost of Blue Prism is too high

99. Explain Selenium VS RPA.

Selenium	RPA
Automates testing of web application	Automates business processes such as maintenance of records, queries, transaction processing, calculation and so on.
Can automate only the current web page.	Can automates all the backend processes that are time-consuming.
Does not support the clerical processes taking place because it works on the front end of the web application.	Helps in maintaining huge records of data and simplify the process and it is flexible in dealing with the clerical processes.

100. How can you differentiate RPA from Macros?

RPA	Macros
Learns and enhances itself from the repetitive process	Does not learns from the repetitive process
Can act Autonomously	Cannot act autonomously
Responds to external stimuli and reprograms	Does not respond to external stimuli.

itself	
Highly secured automation	Security is not a high priority here

101. Can Selenium be used for robotic process automation?

No, Selenium can't be used for RPA. Selenium and RPA are two completely different things and only RPA Tools can deliver process automation solutions.

Selenium is a Web Application Testing tool whereas Robotic Process automation technology is used to automate repeated tasks which involve web and desktop applications.

102. What tool is best for virtual automation?

UI path is the best tool for virtual automation.

103. Which provides open platform for automation in RPA?

TagUI is an open source and free to use RPA tool that is great for web automations.

104. What is abbreviation of WSDL, UDDI, SOAP?

WSDL- Web services Description language

UDDI-Universal description discovery and integration

SOAP- Simple objects access protocol.

105. What is an API?

An application programming interface (API) is an interface or communication protocol between a client and a server intended to simplify the building of client-side software. It has been described as a "contract" between the client and the server, such that if the client makes a request in a specific format, it will always get a response in a specific format or initiate a defined action.

An API may be for a web-based system, operating system, database system, computer hardware, or software library.

An API specification can take many forms, but often includes specifications for routines, data structures, object classes, variables, or remote calls. POSIX, Windows API and ASPI are examples of different forms of APIs.

Please check this out:

Our other best-selling books are-

500+ Java & J2EE Interview Questions & Answers-Java & J2EE Programming

200+ Frequently Asked Interview Questions & Answers in iOS Development

200 + Frequently Asked Interview Q & A in SQL, PL/SQL, Database Development & Administration

200+ Frequently Asked Interview Questions & Answers in Manual Testing

200+ Frequently Asked Interview Q & A in Python Programming

100+ Frequently Asked Interview Q & A in Cyber Security

100+ Frequently Asked Interview Questions & Answers in Scala

100+ Frequently Asked Interview Q & A in Swift Programming

100+ Frequently Asked Interview Questions & Answers in Android Development

Frequently asked Interview Q & A in Java programming

Frequently Asked Interview Questions & Answers in J2EE

Frequently asked Interview Q & A in Angular JS

Frequently asked Interview Q & A in Database Testing

Frequently asked Interview Q & A in Mobile Testing

Frequently asked Interview Q & A in Test Automation-Selenium Testing

Frequently asked Interview Questions & Answers in JavaScript

Frequently Asked Interview Questions & Answers in HTML5

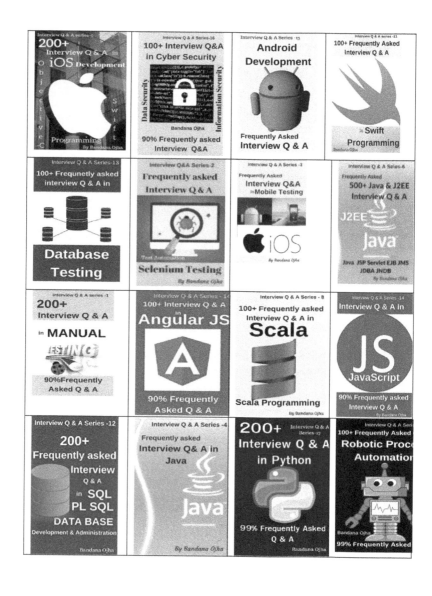

www.ingramcontent.com/pod-product-compliance
Lightning Source LLC
Chambersburg PA
CBHW031249050326
40690CB00007B/1025